D1552987

Victory...in the name of JESUS
©2021 Evangelist Uneala

Proudly self-published by Evangelist Uneala

For permission requests, please contact the author at: evangelistuneala@gmail.com

Unless otherwise noted, Scripture quotations are taken from the Holy bible, King James Version, KJV, Copyright ©2017 by Christian Art Publishers.

Scripture quotations marked NKJV are from the NKJV Bible, The Holy Bible, New King James Version, Copyright © 1979 by Thomas Nelson, Inc.

Scripture quotations taken from the Holy Bible, *New International Version®, NIV®*, Copyright © 1973, 1978, 1984, 2011 by Biblica, Inc. ®
Used by permission. All rights reserved worldwide.

Scripture quotations marked ESV are from the English Standard Version. Public Domain.

Scripture quotations marked NLT are from the New Living Translation Version. Public Domain.

Any names, personal quotes, personal testimonies, or other information printed in this book are offered as a resource and are not intended in any way to insult or to imply endorsement by Evangelist Uneala.

ISBN: 9798457594340
Imprint: Independently Published

DEDICATION:

**THIS HOLY SPIRIT GUIDED BOOK IS DEDICATED TO
MY LORD AND SAVIOR JESUS CHRIST**

**"For whosoever will save his life shall lose it; but whosoever
shall lose his life for my sake and the gospel's, the same shall
save it." – Mark 8:35**

Jesus is my example in suffering. He is my example for living. I
can turn to Him for strength to continue on my journey, my
mission for God. When I suffer for Jesus, He comes to walk me
through it. He is my Savior. This book is only possible because
God allowed it to be possible. I am nothing and can do nothing
without Him.

**"Yea, and all that will live godly in Christ Jesus shall suffer
persecution"
- 2 Timothy 3:12**

**"Therefore I take pleasure in infirmities, in reproaches, in needs,
in persecutions, in distresses, for Christ's sake. For when I am
weak, then I am strong." 2 Corinthians 12:10**

**"When they hurled their insults at Him, He did not retaliate;
when He suffered, He made no threats. Instead, He entrusted
Himself to Him who judges justly." 1 Peter 2:23 - NIV**

**"Jesus saith unto him, I am the way, the truth, and the life: no
man cometh unto the Father, but by me. If ye had known me, ye
should have known my Father also: and from henceforth ye
know Him, and have seen Him." – John 14:6-7**

"Ye have not chosen me, but I have chosen you, and ordained you, that ye should go and bring forth fruit, and that your fruit should remain: that whatsoever ye shall ask of the Father in my name, He may give it you." - John 15:16

I Love You JESUS!

THANK YOU FOR CHOOSING ME

INTRODUCTION

GOD IS INTENTIONAL IN EVERYTHING HE DOES

"Know ye that the LORD He is God: It is He that hath made us, and not we ourselves; we are His people, and the sheep of His pasture." – Psalm 100:3

"But you are a chosen people, a royal priesthood, a holy nation, God's special possession, that you may declare the praises of Him who called you out of darkness into His wonderful light." 1 Peter 2:9 NIV

God created you; you are His. He wants you chasing after Him and giving Him glory. God wants you to live in peace here on earth and in His eternal Kingdom. He wants you saved, baptized, and fill with His Holy Spirit. God has promised that you will be a great nation; He has promised to prosper you; He has promised you hope and peace, not evil; He has promised to send His Son Jesus back for you. All you have to do is HOLD ON...HOLD ON TO HOPE.

"Now hope does not disappoint, because the love of God has been poured out in our hearts by the Holy Spirit, who was given to us." – Romans 5:5 NKJV

I've been fortunate enough to have experienced being in the presence of God. I must tell you, there is absolutely nothing like it in this world; Because of this experience, I continuously long to be in the presence of God. I'm chasing after Him.

When you feel as though you can't make it anymore, cry out to God. When it seem as though everyone around you has turned their backs on you, cry out to God. When it feels like life has taken you on a never ending rollercoaster ride, buckle up...hold on...and cry out to God. He is your stronghold. Jesus gave you access to God through His death on the cross. Because of His death, you have access to God's Holy Spirit and to opportunity for eternal life. Because of Jesus' sacrifice and love for you, He deserves your heart. He keeps His covenant so you should do the same.

 "Know therefore that the LORD thy God, He is God, the faithful God, which keeps covenant and mercy with them that love Him and keep His commandments to a thousand generations; " – Deuteronomy 7:9

From Genesis to Revelations, no one has ever encountered God and walked away saying they are the same or that they did not benefit from the encounter.

GOD IS INTENTIONAL IN EVERYTHING HE DOES

TABLE OF CONTENTS

JOURNEY TO CHRIST...GOD IS ALWAYS THERE

"²²The faithful love of the LORD never ends. His mercies never cease. ²³Great is His faithfulness; His mercies begin afresh each morning. ²⁴I say to myself, the LORD is my inheritance; therefore, I will hope in him." - Lamentations 3:22-24 NLT

Jesus is at the right hand of our Father, in His presence, interceding on your behalf. (Romans 8:34; Hebrews 7:25)

Growing up in the countryside where I picked blackberries, plums, and figs from fields and along roadsides, God was always there. He's always there.

My very first memory is of myself walking barefoot, with no shirt, wearing blue bloomers with small white polka dots. I was born in the sixties so, I believe bloomers are now called underpants. I recall having red bloomers just like the blue one. I see myself walking across a large field which was probably the field between my Bama's house and my Aunt's house. Walking seemed rather new to me so I gather I was learning to walk and was no more than 1 year old. This is where my story begins.

My very next memory is very traumatic. It's of me being molested by a male relative who was left to babysit my siblings and I. I was approximately four years old. God was there... because I made it through. He's always there.

Although you may face abuse and other challenges in this life, God promises to be there with you always. This promise is found in Hebrews 13:5. Our challenges in life are to make us better, not bitter. This type of abuse is the first that I recall but unfortunately, not the last. But God was there with me though it all. He promises to be there for you as well.

God is always there.

"The Lord gives strength to His people; the LORD blesses His people with peace." Psalm 29:11 NIV

"The LORD is good, a strong hold in the day of trouble; and He knoweth them that trust in Him." Nahum 1:7

My very first memory was of a happy carefree toddler. I have joy in that! I am grateful to have this as my first memory, rather than the second. God was there for them both. I too, am grateful for that. He's always there.

Jesus tells us in the Gospel of John 16:33 "These things I have spoken unto you, that in me ye might have peace. In the world ye shall have tribulation: but be of good cheer; I have overcome the world."

God was there when as a child, I found myself on the floorboard in the backseat of a vehicle calling out to the LORD as it drove at a very high speed and eventually stopped at the edge of a cliff. So you see troubles you will have. God didn't promise that you would have no trials or tribulations. He promises to be with you during your troubles and that in Him, you will have peace.

In Deuteronomy 31:6, God tells us to "Be strong and of good courage, fear not, nor be afraid of them: for the

LORD thy God, He it is the One who goes with thee; He will not leave thee, nor forsake thee."

God is always there.

He was there with me when I went out on my search of plums from a tree in an isolated wooded area. I was looking for plums but instead found a large snake hissing up at me. God was there. I didn't know it nor did I understand it at that time, but He was there. I know this because I made it through. I was a babe enjoying the countryside and the trees that bore much fruit. However, I wasn't where I was supposed to be. And when you're not where you are supposed to be, you can count on your adversary Satan, being there. But God was there for me. He's always there.

"⁴Unto the upright there ariseth light in the darkness; He is gracious and full of compassion, and righteous. ⁶Surely he shall not be moved forever: the righteous shall be in everlasting remembrance. ⁷He shall not be afraid of evil tidings: his heart is fixed, trusting in the LORD." Psalm 112:4, 6-7

God is always there.

Call out to Him in your times of need and He will show Himself. He will show up and show out for you. God's true in His promise to never leave you, nor forsake you. Trust Him with your life.

Think about a time or two…or three, when something miraculous or unexpected happened and you couldn't explain it. It defied logic. Think about a time when you said, something told me to do this or something told me not to do that. Well, that something was God's Holy Spirit who is with you here on earth to protect you, to lead you and to guide you in the way you should go. It may have been unexpected for some, but when you have Jesus in your heart, you know and understand that miracles happen every day. You understand that the Holy Spirit is your helper. When the Holy Spirit is nudging you, don't ignore Him; obey Him. I promise that if you do, troubles and tribulations you will avoid and the enemy will have no chance at interrupting your life. You will have put Satan thee behind you. God is here through His Holy Spirit to help you. Take advantage of this spiritual blessing. God has told you that He would never leave you.

God is always there.

I recall having breakfast early mornings with my grandmother Bama after getting eggs from the chicken coop. I didn't of course go inside the coop because I was afraid that the chickens would peck me with their sharp beaks, so I watched. I also sometimes watched as the chickens laid and hatched eggs and remember the warm feel of the eggs after they were laid.

Breakfast consisted of buttered bread and Maxwell House Coffee with lots of sugar and cream. Butter at that time, was usually left on the center of the table along with sugar and napkins so it was soft and easy to spread. There was no toasting; just buttered bread. The coffee was creamy and sweet, just the way Bama liked it. While eating and drinking, we listened to old gospel songs on the radio. And when we weren't listening to it, Bama was humming her favorite tune... "I know a Man from Galilee."

After breakfast, there were house cleaning chores to be done and appointments to go to downtown. But no matter what needed to be done, we were home before soap opera time. The Edge of Night is one show that I recall. Bama would talk with Mrs. Mamie on the phone throughout the day. They talked about the shows; they talked about things going on around town; but most of all, they talked about the LORD.

So, my Bama gave me an early start to my journey to Christ. I was blessed by time shared with her and I can truly appreciate her introducing me to "the Man from Galilee," our Savior Jesus.

The wisdom I took from Bama is both irreplaceable and unforgettable. There's nothing else like it. Proverbs 8:11 tells us "For wisdom is better than rubies; And all the things that may be desired are not to be compared to it."

Growing up as a child with my parents, I went to church because I was made to go, but I actually liked going. However, I don't recall much that I learned from my time in Sunday school and worship service. It's not that it wasn't being taught; I just don't remember. I'm not sure if it's due to the trauma I experienced or if it's because I was more focused on going to buy candy after church. Reciting Easter speeches and singing on the Sunbeam and Junior choirs are what I remember most. These were happy and enjoyable experiences. I do know that Proverbs 22:6 reminds us to "Train up a child in the way he should go: And when he is old, he will not depart from it." I have not departed. The Word of God has sustained me. He gives me strength. He gives me power to endure everything that I face. I am nothing without Him! I can do nothing without Him. This journey to Christ hasn't been easy, but delightful nonetheless.

"I can do all things through Christ which strengthens me." - Philippians 4:13. For Christ is my Rock; the solid rock on which I stand. Praise His Holy Name.

God is always there.

God was there when in elementary school I was sitting on the floor next to my class after returning from Christmas break. As an all "A" student who loved school, I was eager for class to begin. As I sat there, a girl who teased me daily about being poor and living in a ragged house came by and snatched my new cap from my head. This red and blue sweater cap was the only thing I got for Christmas other than fruits and nuts in a brown paper bag. I went to the office to report it.

My mother, who was working hard to help support our family, had to take time away from work to come to the school and confirm my story. Lost work, lost wages. This little girl was the same one who along with her sister and friends, stood on the bathroom toilet and peeked over the stall while I used the restroom. God reminds us in Hebrews 13:5 that He will never leave us nor forsake us.

God is always there.

God was there when I was bullied in eighth grade pre-algebra class. My teacher was totally ok with me, an "A" student, dropping from an "A" to a "D." I loved math; it was my favorite subject. I was bullied so badly that after pleading to my teacher with no results, all I knew to do was put my head down on my desk and wait for class to be over. I grew tired of asking the teacher to ask this young man to leave me alone, only to have her do nothing about it. She witnessed it day after day. During those days students sat in alphabetical order. My last name began with "P" while his began with "M." There were no switching seats however, I did ask. But even after witnessing my torment, this teacher refused. This experience changed the course of my life! Instead of being my favorite subject, math was now my most feared and avoided. My confidence was shattered; my esteem was shattered; my trust in school authority was shattered. So instead of retaking pre-algebra in ninth grade, I ran from it.

God is always there.

"15For you did not receive a spirit that makes you a slave again to fear, but you received the spirit of Sonship. And by Him we cry, 16Abba Father, The Spirit Himself testifies with our spirit that we are God's children." – Romans 8:15-16.

"For the Lord your God is He that goes with you, to fight for you against your enemies, to save you." Deuteronomy 20:4

Finishing high school and college, and then going on to pursue other endeavors, I found myself going to church on my own terms. There was no one to make me go but there was someone urging me to go. That someone was God's Holy Spirit and I'm so glad He did. God was always there. As a young adult, I began focusing more on God. When I did, I began to notice Him showing up exactly when I needed Him most. He really is an on time God. He shows you in Romans 8:39 that nothing in all creation will be able to separate you from His love.

God is always there.

I recall struggling to pay bills; calling out to the Lord and praying for Him to help me during my times of need. God showed up every time. He showed me that He would always be there and that I could always trust Him. I stood in amazement of my blessings...thinking, what a mighty God we serve. Exactly what I needed was either in the mailbox, in my bank account, or given to me by someone whom God used to do His Will. Oh yes! He will use others to do His will even when they're not aware that God is using them. Only God could have known and made it all possible...only God!

God is always there.

There were times I found myself in places and situations I should not have been in. God was there; He brought me out.

God was there in good times and in bad. He was there when at age 23 I gave birth to my first child and the pain got so bad that I told Him I give up. I was ready to see Jesus. He was there when at age 23 I was diagnosed with cervical cancer cells. He was there when at age 23, my Dad died suddenly. These traumatic events all took place within a matter of months. My baby girl was just four months old when "Da" died. This was all traumatic and a bit much for one to handle in the flesh. No wonder Satan tried to steal my mind...but God was there!

"Consider it pure joy, my brothers and sisters when you face trials of many kinds, because you know that the testing of your faith produce perseverance." – James 1:2 NIV

I've experienced many hard times and sacrifices but through it all, God was there. Going through times like divorce, you find out who your true friends are and which family members truly love and support you. And if you're still not sure, receive and accept your calling from God to preach His word – you will definitely know for sure. <u>Unlike</u> in the Old Testament of the Bible, messengers of God today are not as revered. Neither are they as humbled. But this must not deter us messengers. We must pray and press on to do the will of God.

"But Jesus said unto them, "A prophet is not without honor, except in his own country, and among his own kin, and in his own house." Mark 6:4

God is always there.

Through my growth with, God I've learned to not take anything personal. I've learned to not allow others to make their issues, my issues. Just because you have mess going on within you and around you, you don't get to take it out on me or to make your issues about me. You don't get to steal my joy. God gives it to me each day and each day I choose to receive it, to live in it, and to enjoy every moment of it.

If you choose to live in misery and self hatred through the evilness that you display, then do it without involving others who choose joy; who choose to live in peace; who choose to be positive and live as Jesus would have us live...enjoying peace in His presence and loving all of His people.

I am glad to be a friend of God's; to be called a friend of God, who follows His commands.

"[14]Ye are my friends, if ye do whatsoever I command you. [15]Henceforth I call you not servants: for the servant knows not what his lord does: but I have called you friends; for all things that I have heard of my Father I have made known unto you. "John 15:14-15.

A WAY OUT...LOVE BROUGHT ME BACK

Jehovah Makadesh – My Sanctifier

"Love bears all things, believes all things, hopes all things, endures all things." - 1 Corinthians 13:7 ESV

My daughter gave me something once that says, "Life takes us to unexpected places...Love brings us home." – Melissa McClone

Jesus is the Messiah...my Deliverer...my Sanctifier.

Having experienced what I thought was the worst thing that could ever happen to me in my adult life, I was looking for a way out. As a result, I chose divorce because my heart was hardened. I felt justified because I had chosen a worldly husband of whom I was not equally yoked. I felt justified because I had chosen a husband for myself, rather than allowing God to choose for me, a godly man. I felt justified because my husband brought home something he did not leave home with and because adultery was a way of life for Him. Because I did not focus on God, I wasn't a righteous woman who submitted herself to her husband because I didn't deem him worthy. My focus

22

was not on God, so I did not reverence husband as lord, as Sarah did with Abraham. Pride was a factor. I went to church but I did not live for Christ. I was not loved as Christ loved the church so I did not submit myself to Christ or to my husband. There are just too many I's in this passage. When "I" become more than "my God," it's no longer about God.

A way out...love brought me back

Ephesians 5:22-25 says [22]"Wives, submit yourselves unto your own husbands, as unto the LORD. [23]For the husband is the head of the wife, even as Christ is the head of the church: and He is the Saviour of the body. [24]Therefore as the church is subject unto Christ, so let the wives be to their own husbands in everything. [25]Husbands, love your wives, even as Christ also loved the church, and gave himself for it;"

When you choose your husband or your wife for yourself rather than allowing God to choose, you end up looking for a way out as I did. It takes two spiritually healthy people to maintain a spiritually healthy marriage.

2 Corinthians 6:14 tells us to "Be ye not unequally yoked together with unbelievers: for what fellowship hath righteousness with unrighteousness? And what communion hath light with darkness?"

You have to understand the word of God and have spiritual discernment to be able to recognize darkness when it comes your way. And when you do recognize it, you must not settle for less and ignore it. God loves you and values you; you are a chosen people, made in His image. So why would you allow anyone to treat you as other than who God says you are. When you recognize darkness...do not commune with it...stay away. Find wisdom, which the LORD says is more precious than jewels.

A way out...Love brought me back

Seeking God and His divine intervention without fully knowing and trusting Him will lead you to looking for a way out.

Regardless of who you choose to marry, when you're focused on your husband's or your wife's faults and flaws instead of on God and His mighty power, you begin to look for a way out.

When your focus is on how bad your situation is instead of how big your God is, you begin to look for a way out. God says in Jeremiah 17:7 "Blessed is the man that trusted on the LORD, and whose hope the LORD is."

In the Gospel of Matthew 11:28 He says, "Come unto me, all ye that labour and are heavy laden (burdened), and I will give you rest." He says "cast thy burden upon the LORD and He will sustain thee: he shall never suffer the righteous to be moved." Psalm 55:22

When you feel as though you need a way out, this is the time to trust and totally depend on God, not your own understanding. This is the time to fully rely on Him. My favorite yogurt shop is Sweet F.R.O.G. (Fully Rely on God). It's amazing what we go through before actually getting to the point of fully relying on God.

There is nothing new under the sun. So why then, must you taste dirt for yourselves to know that it doesn't taste good? Why then must you try to reinvent a wheel that is not broken?

Why? Because you are like Missouri the show me state. You don't believe sugar is sweet until you taste it for yourself. It's not enough to know that fire burns, you need to feel it, only to discover that it doesn't feel good. Jesus is and always will be the answer, no matter the question. He is peace; He is Joy; He is the way out.

Knowing and trusting that God loves you, keeps you and brings you back in right standing with Him. Praying and trusting God to answer your prayers and to give you the desires of your heart brings you back.

"Confess your faults one to another, and pray for one another, that ye may be healed. The effectual fervent prayer of a righteous man availeth much." - James 5:16

Powerful things happen when you call on the name of Jesus. Don't look for the easiest or the quickest way out of a situation. Look for God's way. His way is and always will be the best. Job 28:23 reminds us that "God understands the way we should go, and He knows the place where we should go." God knows what you are going through. He knows all and sees all. Jesus came to live on earth to both experience and understand everything you face. He literally walked in your shoes!

2 Samuel 22:31 says "As for God, His way is perfect; the word of the LORD is tried: He is a buckler to all those that trust in Him." The LORD's way is tried so He knows and understands. You don't have to experience unnecessary trials.

Don't look for a way out. Look for God and let love bring you back. The word of God is tried; it's been tested and it is true. You don't need to test it again. God says to trust Him in all circumstances. I did not F.R.O.G., Fully rely on God but I am right where He would have me to be, in His perfect peace.

"A man's heart deviseth his way: but the LORD directs his steps." Proverbs 16:9

"The steps of a good man are ordered by the LORD: and he delighteth in his way." Psalm 37:23

I am stepping with Jesus, fully relying on God, doing as Colossians 3:2 says, to set my minds on things above. God has to be number one in individual lives to maintain both individual and relationship happiness. You cannot reply on others to fulfill you. You cannot change someone's heart. Only God can do that.

God has to be your everything: Your bread; your water; your light; your everything.

And Jesus said unto them, "I am the bread of life: he that cometh to me shall never hunger; and he that believeth on me shall never thirst." – John 6:35

"As long as I am in the world, I am the light of the world." – John 9:5

"I am the LORD, your Holy One, the Creator of Israel, your King."- Isaiah 43:15

Believe in God, not man. Trust in God, not man. God will never disappoint you. Jesus is your defense so live not in fear, but in F.R.O.G., fully relying on God.

EXPECT NOTHING FROM MAN; EVERYTHING FROM GOD

El Shaddai – My Provider

"For we brought nothing into this world, and it is certain we can carry nothing out." 1 Timothy 6:7

You are best when you expect nothing. Therefore, expect nothing from this ole sinful, temporal world.

 If you expect nothing but you receive something, then it's all good because you receive without expecting to receive. If you expect nothing and you receive nothing, you are still good because you didn't expect anything.

People will let you down. You can count on it. You can expect as much as you want to from others but you only have control of yourself. You cannot make nor can you expect others to be who you want them to be or do as you would have them to do. If you want disappointments, expect much! If you want joy and a peace that transcends all understanding, put your faith and trust in God. He will never let you down.

"But let patience have her perfect work, that ye may be perfect and entire, wanting nothing." James 1:4

God knows not only what you need, but He knows what you want. So you can expect Him to give you the desires of our heart when you trust in Him. Psalm 37:4 tells us to "Delight thyself also in the LORD; And He shall give thee the desires of thine heart." Delight thyself! Take great pleasure in pleasing the Lord and watch Him show up in your life, giving you all that you desire and more.

This sinful world brings torment, broken dreams, and wishful thinking. Delighting yourselves in the LORD brings you joy, peace and fulfillment like none other. Jesus fills you up so that you're not depleted from expectations.

God created you to walk in His light; enjoying peace that only He can give. He wants this for you. Be content with all that He blesses you with. Hebrews 13:5 reminds you to be content with what you have.

Expect nothing from man; everything from God

"[34] And when He had called the people unto Him with His disciples also, He said unto them, "whosoever will come after me, let him deny himself, and take up his cross, and follow me. [35]For whoever will save his life shall lose it; but whoever shall lose his life for my sake and the gospels, the same shall save it. [36] For what shall it profit a man, if he shall gain the whole world, and lose his own soul? [37] Or what shall a man give in exchange for his soul? [38] Whosoever therefore shall be ashamed of me and of my words in this adulterous and sinful generation; of him also shall the Son of man be ashamed, when He cometh in the glory of His Father with the Holy angels." Mark 8:34-38

It doesn't matter what others do or what path they take, you must do what God asks and requires of you. Jesus knows the way...we only need to follow Him.

"My only aim is to finish the race and complete the task the LORD Jesus has given me." Acts 20:24

JESUS IS THE ANSWER, NO MATTER THE QUESTION

Jehovah – My LORD God

"For God so loved the world that He gave His only begotten Son that whosoever believeth in Him, shall not perish, but have everlasting life." John 3:16

"Salvation is found in no one else, for there is no other name under heaven given to men by which we must be saved." – Acts 4:12

Love, which is a powerful expression of both feeling and commitment, should not be taken lightly or regarded casually.

That faithful day in Golgotha, outside Jerusalem, they hung Him high and stretched Him wide...that's love.

Consider how 2 Corinthians 5:21 tells us that Jesus had never sinned and how 1 Peter 2:22 says that there was no fault found in Him...Jesus was guilty of nothing, yet He was crucified, dead, and buried for you and for me; for your sins and for mine...that's love.

So the answer to any problem you may be facing right now is Jesus.

Jesus is the answer, no matter the question. You can ALWAYS turn to Him and Jesus will supply ALL your needs. The answer is and will forever be with HIM. It doesn't matter if you feel you're being treated unfairly, or got overlooked for a job or a promotion, have lost a loved one, having trouble conceiving, have been the victim or the suspect of a crime, Jesus is the answer. He will love you when it seems like no one else will. He loves you at your best; He loves you at your worst. He loves you unconditionally-without restrictions or restraints.

"But God commendeth His love towards us, in that, while we were yet sinners, Christ died for us." – Romans 5:8

Jesus is the answer, no matter the question

You must love all people; We are all God's people. "He that loveth not knoweth not God; for God is love. 1 John 4:8

If you can love all people, you can forgive all things. 1 Peter 4:8 tells us "And above all things have fervent (passionate or glowing) charity (love) among yourselves: for charity (love) shall cover the multitude of sins."

Jesus is perfect love. He is your example of how you are to love. He came to live here on earth so that you would not have to guess at it. He came to show you how to love as He loves. In the gospel of Matthew 22:37-40, Jesus gives you His two greatest commandments. "[37] "Jesus said unto him, Thou shalt love the LORD thy God with all thy heart, and with all thy soul, and with all thy mind. [38] This is the first and great commandment. [39] And the second is like unto it, Thou shalt love thy neighbor as thyself. [40] On these two commandments hang all the law and the prophets."

Why do we hang all the law and the prophets on these two commandments? BECAUSE LOVE IS THE ANSWER, NO MATTER THE QUESTION.

Love can and will do what nothing else in the world can do. Love will make even your enemies love you - love beareth all things – love can turn things around in your life when you can see no way out – love will make your enemies your footstool – love always wins! Jesus is Love. Jesus tells you in the sixth chapter of the gospel of Luke to love your enemies and do good by them and your reward will be great and you shall be the children of the Highest. Love really does conquer all.

Jesus is the answer, no matter the question

I know that it is not always easy to love everyone. But I promise you that the more you try, the easier it becomes. Anything is possible to the one who believes. When you are sincerely trying to live in God's light, He will shine His light brightly upon you and direct your steps. If you trust Him and follow Him, before you know it, loving even your enemies will become second nature and you will be left to wonder, why isn't everyone seeking to live in God's light?

Jesus is the answer, no matter the question

Choose to live in the light of love…God's light. In Him, there is no darkness. Do not deceive yourselves into believing that the evilness you engage in has anything to do with God's love. Hatred, spitefulness, gossiping, backbiting, strife, and simply put, messiness, is of darkness. In it there is no light.

Again, God is light: And in Him, there is no darkness. Darkness doesn't comprehend light. Wouldn't you rather lift someone up rather than tear them down?

Jesus is the answer, no matter the question. Jesus is love. "Then Jesus spoke unto them, saying, I am the light of the world: he that followeth Me shall not walk in darkness, but shall have the light of life." – John 8:12

"Ye are the light of the world. A city that is set on a hill cannot be hid." – Matthew 5:14

Let your light so shine – your light of love. Let it radiate your beauty, showing all that God designed and assigned you to be. Be focused on and remain focused on the light of love. It doesn't matter how dark it looks in your situation or how dark things may seem in your life right now; focus on God and His light will shine forth. "He made us, and we are His. We are His people, the sheep of His pasture." – Psalm 100:3

Jesus is the answer, no matter the question

Jesus didn't sacrifice His life for you only to give up on you. He loves you and never gives up on you. He is always the answer.

Our words are powerful. They have the power to kill and the power to give life. Love is a commitment; to God, to self, and to our neighbors (others). Don't regard it casually, for God knows your heart. Your goal should be to have love in your heart for everyone. For when you do, it pleases God. For when you do, you can accept Jesus as your Savior.

You don't need to do anything to earn God's love. You don't deserve it but you don't have to earn it either. Jesus' love for you has paid your sinful debt. He paid in full with His life on the cross in Calvary. Love Him because He first loved you. Love others because you are all God's children and because God commands you to.

[10] "If ye keep my commandments, ye shall abide in my love; even as I have kept my Father's commandments, and abide in His love. "[11]These things have I spoken unto you, that my joy might remain in you, and that your joy might be full." – John 15:10-11

Oh how I love Jesus...because He first loved me. He is the Messiah; the answer to all of your questions.

Rest in the Lamb of God.

OBEDIENCE IS BETTER THAN SACRIFICE

Jehovah – My LORD God

¹³ "Just as it is written in the Law of Moses, all this disaster has come on us, yet we have not sought the favor of the LORD our God by turning from our sins and giving attention to His truth. ¹⁴ The LORD did not hesitate to bring the disaster on us, for the LORD our God is righteous in everything He does; yet we have not obeyed Him." - Daniel 9:13-14

"And Samuel said, Does the LORD delight in burnt offerings and sacrifices as much as in obeying the LORD? To obey is better than sacrifice, and to heed is better than the fat of rams." - 1 Samuel 15:22

In other words, more than your money, more than your time spent doing good deeds, or anything else that may be a sacrifice to you, the LORD wants you to obey Him. He wants you to listen for the voice of His Holy Spirit and to do what it says. God wants you to do things His way. He wants all of you living by His word standards, not the world standards.

The LORD speaks to you through His Word in the Holy Bible. He speaks to you through His Holy Spirit whom He graciously gave to you here on earth. He speaks to you through wise counsel from your parents and elders and pastors and mentors and friends, and even through the laws of the land. We must obey.

James 1:22 tells us "Do not merely listen to the word, and so deceive yourselves. Do what it says."

Obedience is better than sacrifice

[20]"Children, obey your parents in all things: For this is well pleasing unto the LORD. [21] Fathers, provoke not your children to anger, lest they be discouraged." - Colossians 3:20-21

Parents and children are to be obedient to God's word – to each other.

I recall as a child growing up, when I was not obedient to my parents, there were consequences and sacrifices. My bottom was sacrificed more times than I care to remember. As an adult, the consequences of my actions are hard lessons learned: time lost with God, abusive and broken relationships and friendships, painful and shameful memories.

Obedience is better than sacrifice

Disobedience causes you to be out of line with God. Disobedience can be found in behaviors such as selfish desires, pride, stubbornness, hatred, unforgiveness and just plain ole evilness. You have to be careful not to allow these things to manifest and fester in your spirit. For when they do, your adversary is most delightful. When you do, you open a window or door of opportunity for him to come in. Once he's in, he won't stop until he steals your joy, kills your spirit, and destroys your relationships.

The gospel of John 10:10 tells you that "The thief cometh not, but for to steal, and to kill, and to destroy: I am come that they might have life, and that they might have it more abundantly." See how much God loves you. He's always there to protect you. You just need to make room for Him in your hardened hearts.

Obedience is better than sacrifice

You have to trust God one day at a time so you can live in His peace, one day at a time. "Boast not thyself of tomorrow; for thou knoweth not what a day may bring forth." - Proverbs 27:1

You do not know what will happen tomorrow. Only God does. This is why you must put your trust in Him. We all have our own struggles and because we do, we often handle them in ways that not only affect ourselves, but the lives of others as well. This is why we are instructed to take everything to the LORD in prayer. When you have the pressures of life...family, health, finance, and other issues, they can sometimes become overwhelming and a bit much for you to handle responsibly and respectfully when we depend on our own understanding; when you trust flesh instead of God's Holy Spirit. This is why you should keep the word of God in our heart at all times. It helps you to be obedient, no matter the sacrifice. You shouldn't mind a sacrifice for the LORD.

In this way, you don't attempt to handle your struggles by mistreating others or yourselves with toxins such as alcohol or drugs, sexual behaviors, over eating and destructive relationships. Don't make your issues, other people issues. They're yours! Own them and then do something about them. If you're not happy with your life, don't take it out on someone else. Seek Jesus!

God promises to love, provide for and protect you. He tells you in Hebrews 4:16, "Let us then approach the throne of grace with confidence, so that we may receive mercy and find grace to help us in our time of need." God wants to help you. He tells you in Psalm 55:22 to "Give your burdens to the LORD, and He will take care of you." There's nothing more you need.

Life with God is about obedience. Abiding will bring you so much joy. Defying (disobedience) will bring you just the opposite...a life of unnecessary heartache and pain.

Obedience is better than sacrifice

God intentionally tells you "If my people, which are called by my name, shall humble themselves, and pray, and seek my face, and turn from their wicked ways; then will I hear from heaven, and will forgive their sin, and will heal their land." 2 Chronicles 7:14

Imagine everyone here on earth following these intentional instructions from God; what a wonderful world it would be.

Obedience is better than sacrifice

Here is what God wants to do for you...

"Make you perfect in every good work to do His will, working in you that which is well pleasing in His sight, through Jesus Christ; to whom be glory forever and ever. Amen" – Hebrews 13:21

GOD IS IN THE BUSINESS OF HEALING

Jehovah Rophe – My Healer

[13]"Christ hath redeemed us from the curse of the law, being made a curse for us; for it is written, cursed is every one that hangeth on a tree, [14]that the blessing of Abraham might come on the Gentiles through Jesus Christ; that we might receive the promise of the Spirit through Faith" – Galatians 3:13-14

"Jesus said unto him, if thou canst believe, all things are possible to him that believeth."

Humble yourselves before the LORD. If you need healing, bow down and cry out to Him. Psalm 30:2 says "Oh LORD my God, I cried out to you, and you healed me."

Jeremiah said, save me LORD and I will be saved; Heal me LORD and I will be healed. Jeremiah had faith! This is the kind of faith you need for your healing. Jesus redeemed us. We don't have to live in our sickness, illness, and diseases. Believe that you are healed and you are.

"Confess your faults one to another and pray one for another, that ye may be healed. The effectual fervent prayer of a righteous man availeth much." – James 5:16 You are accountable for how you live. Jesus is LORD to everyone and to all things because He created all things.

Sickness, illness, and disease are of darkness. They are of Satan himself. God represents light. Jesus is the light of the world; A light upon our pathways. Darkness was not God's way from the beginning of time. God created a perfect world and a perfect man and gave him the tree of life. In the second chapter of the book of Genesis, we learn that God placed the tree of life in the midst of the Garden of Eden. Man had full access to the tree of life. God also gives us free will. This is why obedience is so important.

Obedience is very important to God and is crucial on your journey with the LORD and for your healing process. You must obey God's commands to have access to the tree of life and all that awaits you in His kingdom of Heaven.

Revelation 22:14 tells us "Blessed are they that do His commandments, that they may have right to the tree of life, and may enter in through the gates into the city."

It is God's will that we be healed. God does not bring darkness of sickness, illness, disease, and death upon His children. He brings us in His light of good health, healing, love, unity, and prosperity. God wants to heal you but you must have faith that He can and He will. In the gospel of Luke, chapter 2, those who had faith were healed.

God is in the business of healing

Healing requires obedience. This cannot be stressed enough. Living a life aligned with the word of God, abiding by His commands is how you receive your healing.

Jesus said "But ye shall receive power, after that the Holy Ghost is come upon you: and ye shall be witnesses unto me both in Jerusalem, and in all Judaea, and in Samaria, and unto the uttermost part of the earth." – Acts 1:8

You have power that many of you don't realize you have. So, you accept sickness; you accept disease; you accept defeat; and you accept Satan's lies over your lives. He has been defeated and you have been redeemed. Therefore, the power that Jesus has, you received when He died on the cross. It is God's will that you be obedient. It is God's will that you be healed. Stop allowing Satan to use you and abuse you. Stop allowing him to steal your joy, kill your spirit, and destroy your relationships. I did! I stopped Him; When I totally and completely trusted God for my healing and my blessings, I was freed from the bondage of the evil one. I understood my power, my value and my worth in the name of Jesus. I understand who I am in the LORD. Yes, he, Satan is crafty, BUT GOD has ALL power in His hands. Trust Him for your total and complete healing today.

You have to maintain a close relationship with God, seeking His face and being in His presence so that you can be patient in tribulations, joyful in hope and faithful in prayer as Romans 12:12 tells you.

"Let us draw near to God with a sincere heart and with the full assurance that faith brings." – Hebrews 10:22

"I have told you this so that my joy may be in you and that your joy may be complete." – John 15:11

God has healed me many times of many things: sickness, illness and disease. The devil is a liar! I looked to the LORD from whence my help comes from; the LORD who had healed me many times before; The Lord of whom I can both depend on and trust in.

God is in the business of healing

I no longer live in bondage under the curse of the law. Jesus redeemed me. Jesus restored me. Jesus sanctified my life. His Holy Spirit indwells me. I am blessed beyond measure and you can be too. Trust God with your life. Trust Him for your healing. He is in the business of healing.

When God heals and or delivers you from something, you no longer need treatment from earthly doctors. He is your Chief Physician.

If you, your husband, your wife, your children, or other family members are struggling with health issues and life issues time after time again, try something different. If sickness, illness and disease, keeps knocking on your door, try something different. Try living to please God, rather than self; rather than man.

Ask yourself, am I living a life pleasing to God?

Are you gossiping and backbiting?

"The north wind driveth away rain: so doth an angry countenance a backbiting tongue." - Proverbs 25:23; "Let your conversation be without covetousness; and be content with such things as ye have: for He hath said, I will never leave thee, nor forsake thee." - Hebrews 13:5; "Thou shalt not go up and down as a talebearer among people: neither shall thou stand against the blood of thy neighbor: I am the LORD." – Leviticus 19:16; "He that covert a transgression seeketh love; but he that repeateth a matter separateth very friends." – Proverbs 17:9; Chapter one in Romans warns us about being filled with unrighteousness such as backbiters, haters of God, despiteful, proud, boasters, inventors of evil things, disobedient to parents.

Many of you choose to lie to yourselves by choosing to believe that what you are doing does not fit in this category. Stop fooling yourselves! Every time you pick up that phone to talk about what's going on or what you think is going on in someone else's life, you are gossiping; you are backbiting. Your opinion of what you think of someone else doesn't matter. Rather than talking negatively about a family, pray that God will sustain them and bring them joy. What good does it do you to know what's going on with someone else? It's just more mess to fill you spirit, and less room for God to come in. You know that what you and your friends and or family members are discussing about other people's lives is not pleasing to God. It's gossiping and backbiting. It's unfortunate that this messiness gets passed on to your children to the point they are disrespectful to adults without even realizing they are. They've been privy to too many negative adult conversations. It becomes rooted in their spirits and becomes generational; don't pass your mess onto your children. Parents, you are responsible for how you train up your children as God's word says to train up a child in the way he should go, meaning the way of the LORD, not the evil one. Gossiping and backbiting is of darkness and has absolutely nothing to do with the LORD. You've stopped parenting to become friends with your children and other people's children instead of guiding them in the way of the LORD. If you have an issue with someone, go to them and talk <u>with</u> them, not about them. Many misunderstandings or misjudgments can be resolved this way.

"If your brother sins against you, go and tell him his fault, between you and him alone. If he listens to you, you have gained your brother." – Matthew 18:15

"Brothers, if anyone is caught in any transgression, you who are spiritual should restore him in a spirit of gentleness. Keep watch on yourself, lest you too be tempted." – Galatians 6:1

"Let no corrupt talk come out of your mouths, but only such as is good for building up, as fits the occasion, that it may give grace to those who hear." – Ephesians 4:29

"Therefore encourage one another and build one another up, just as you are doing." – 1 Thessalonians 5:11

Don't allow family, friends, and others to dump their garbage into your lives. Each time someone approaches you with negative talk, with gossip, with backbiting, or with selfishness, don't allow them to dump their sewage; their waste, into your fresh water system. Don't allow them to pollute you. Keep your system clean by filtering what comes in. Keep it clean from dump like garbage and debris. This is how you cleanse and maintain wholeness. Clean it up and watch God clean you up from the inside out! Watch God bless you beyond measure. Remember...people only dump where they know they can. So, you have the power to stop the garbage before it stinks. Don't be a dumping ground for someone else's trash; you're better than that. Be spiritually minded.

"⁶For to be carnally minded is death; but to be spiritually minded is life and peace. ⁷Because the carnal mind is enmity against God: for it is not subject to the law of God, neither indeed can be. [8]So then they that are in the flesh cannot please God." – Romans 8:6-8

God is in the business of healing

Are you jealous or envious of others?

"Charity (love) suffereth long, and is kind; charity (love) envieth not; charity (love) vaunteth not itself, is not puffed up." – 1 Corinthians 13:4

[2]"Ye lust, and have not: ye kill, and desire to have, and cannot obtain: ye fight and war, yet have not, because ye ask not. [3]Ye ask, and receive not, because ye ask amiss, that ye may consume it upon your lusts." – James 4:2-3

"Let nothing be done through strife or vainglory; but in lowliness of mind let each esteem the other better than themselves." – Philippians 2:3

"A sound heart is the life of the flesh: but envy the rottenness of the bones." – Proverbs 14:30

"But if ye have bitter envying and strife in your hearts, glory not, and lie not against the truth." – James 3:14

"For wrath killeth the foolish man, and envy slayeth the silly one." – Job 5:2

Are you mutilating your body with tattoos and other markings and alterations?

"Ye shall not make any cuttings in your flesh for the dead, nor print any marks upon you: I am the LORD." – Leviticus 19:28

When you know better, you do better.

God is in the business of healing

Are you indulging in drunkenness or smoking nicotine and or other harmful substances to your body, which is a temple of the LORD?

"Which are a shadow of things to come; the body is of Christ." – Colossians 2:17

[19] "What? Know ye not that your body is the temple of the Holy Spirit which is in you, which ye have of God, and ye are not your own? [20]For ye are bought with a price: therefore glorify God in your body, and in your spirit, which are God's." – 1 Corinthians 6:19-20

God is in the business of healing

Being faithful church members won't get you your healing. Being a faithful tither won't get you your healing. Being well connected in church, in politics, or in your community won't get you your healing. Jesus heals when you are obedient to His word and when you bow down and cry out to Him. Pride has no place in the healing process. God has told us that we have not because we ask not.

Jesus laid down His life for you and for me. He takes care of His children. Our part is to receive Him and to keep in good relationship with Him by being obedient to His word. This is how you get your healing.

God is in the business of healing

"Therefore, holy brothers, who share in the heavenly calling, fix your thoughts on Jesus, the Apostle and High Priest whom we confess." – Hebrews 3:1

For "Every word of God is pure; He is a shield unto them that put their trust in Him." – Hebrews 30:5

Brokenness cannot be healed until one accepts that there is brokenness to be healed. A problem can only be fixed when there is a problem. Living in denial only causes your issues to manifest longer and deeper into your ungodly spirit. This is why brokenness that cannot physically be seen is causing so much hurt and hardened heart in so many people. You have to surrender to God so that you can be healed.

Being male or female doesn't make you a Kingdom man or a Kingdom woman. Kingdom men and Kingdom women not only fear God, we live for God, a true and righteous life. We seek after Him continuously. This is how we heal. We make God priority in our lives – above ALL else. Jesus tells you in Revelation 3:16 "But

since you are like lukewarm water, neither hot nor cold, I will spit you out of my mouth!"

Are you a Kingdom man or a male?

Are you a Kingdom woman or a female?

The LORD desires fellowship with you. Jesus tells you in Revelation 3:20 "Behold, I stand at the door, and knock: if any man hear my voice, and open the door; I will come in to him, and will come eat with him." A meal signifies fellowship.

If you're going to give God your all and make Him priority in your life, you will have to give up your desire to please other people. Relationship with Christ remains even when earthly friendships fail.

"For those who look to God, their faces are radiant in His light and are never ashamed." Psalm 34:5

If you want your healing, don't be ashamed of God. He tells you in Luke 9:26 that "For whoever is ashamed of me and my words, of him will the Son of Man be ashamed when He comes in His glory ant the glory of the Father and of the Holy Angels."

"Oh my God, I trust in thee: let me not be ashamed, let not mine enemies triumph over me." Psalm 25:2

Rest in the Lamb of God and proclaim your healing today.

"A cheerful heart is good medicine." – Proverbs 17:22

RENOVATE YOUR HEART

Omnipotent – God has ALL Power…He can do anything

Potentate – The <u>power</u> of God to lead you to Salvation; to Restoration

God restores all who accepts His Son Jesus

"And be not conformed to the world: but be ye transformed by the renewing of your mind, that ye may prove what is that good, and acceptable, and perfect, will of God" – Romans 12:2

When Jesus spoke again to the people, he said, "I am the light of the world. Whoever follows me will never walk in darkness, but will have the light of life." – John 8:12

"Depending on God isn't weakness, it's acknowledging His strength."- Anne Cetas

Ask…and it will be given to you.

Seek…and you will find.

Knock…and the door will be opened.

The one who asks receives; the one who seeks, finds; the one who knocks, the door will be opened. When you're connected to the power, you talk differently; you walk differently; you look differently; and you act differently.

Like Joseph in the Old Testament, you too may be betrayed and even face many trials, but know that there's purpose in these trying times; to bring you closer to God. They are part of God's plan for you. Keep in mind Genesis 50:20 what Joseph said to his brothers. "But as for you, you meant evil against me; but God meant it for good, in order to bring it about as it is this day, to save many people alive."

Because of the sacrifice that Joseph unwillingly and unknowingly made, he not only saved his family but he save the people of Egypt, the people of Israel, and people everywhere around the world. Therefore, your trials and tribulations, God too, will use for your good and for the good of others. Worry not about your enemies when you have the right relationship with God and His power. God asks you to love and forgive, even your enemies. This is how you renovate and restore your heart.

I praise God each day for His Holy Spirit leading, guiding, and protecting me. God tells you in the fourth chapter of Proverbs to pay attention to His words, not putting them out of our sight, but keeping them in your hearts. God's word will renew your heart and restore your faith. He created you in His image and that's where He wants you to remain, in His image, in the likeness of Him.

"Let the peace that comes from Christ rule in your hearts. For as members of one body you are called to live in peace." – Colossians 3:15

God is Spirit, so you must worship Him in both spirit and in truth. The Holy Spirit is the Glory of the LORD. Therefore, you must allow Him into your hearts to make the necessary changes so you can become more like Him, in His image. The Holy Spirit indwelling in you is what makes you more like God so invite the Holy Spirit into your heart. He indwelled Jesus while He was on earth and Jesus' heart is the perfect example of how your heart should be: full of love, kindness, compassion, forgiveness, and understanding. God's Holy Spirit should be controlling our every action and thought.

2 Corinthians 3:18 tells us "But we all, with unveiled face, beholding as in a mirror the glory of the LORD, are being transformed into the same image from glory to glory, just as by the Spirit of the LORD."

"Yet to all who did receive Him, to those who believed in His name, He gave the right to become children of God." – John 1:12

Take time to reflect on your life. Is God there in every aspect? If not, then you have some renovating to do. God tells you not to be anxious or to worry about anything. He tells you to bring everything to Him in prayer. Last I checked, everything meant everything, with nothing left out. For when you do, He promises to keep your hearts and minds in perfect peace and supply all of your needs. Nothing is too small or too big for your Mighty God.

"Be careful for nothing; but in everything by prayer and supplication with thanksgiving let your requests be made known unto God. [7]And the peace of God, which passeth all understanding, shall keep your hearts and minds through Christ Jesus." – Philippians 4:6-7

God grants you free will. The decision to accept Jesus as LORD and Savior and to live by the commands of God is yours and yours alone. You will not be forced to believe in Him or accept Him.

"A wise man will hear, and will increase learning; and a man of understanding shall attain unto wise counsels: [6]To understand Proverbs, and the interpretation; the words of the wise, and their dark sayings. [7]The fear of the LORD is the beginning of knowledge: but fools despise wisdom and instruction." – Proverbs 5-7

"Submit yourselves therefore to God. Resist the devil, and he will flee from you." – James 4:7

You are commanded to love one another and to live in peace with one another. The gospel of Matthew tells you that those who work for peace will be called children of God. You are to love one another and have compassion for one another. You do this by seeking to understand each other so you can speak each other's language.

"If you talk to a man in a language he understands, that goes to his head. If you talk to him in his language, that goes to his heart." – Nelson Mandela

It takes a renewed heart to show compassion, to seek understanding, and to put others above self – selfless sacrifice, when you feel they have wronged you or have hurt you. It can be done with the help of the LORD. Once you allow Him into your heart, you live for peace. And there is no peace like the peace of being in the presence of the LORD. I experienced His presence in 2017 after fasting from television for 22 days. I woke up early mornings and read my Bible before going to work. I prayed and spoke with God throughout the day while at work and read again before going to bed at night. At some point nearing the 22nd day, I was awakened approximately 4:00 a.m. by God's Holy Spirit. I was in His light; in His presence. His light shone on my Bible while He delicately like velvet, turned the pages. He stopped and all I could see was John 15:16. I did actually see what the scripture said. Nearing my last hour or so of deep sleep, I had a choice to make. I could be obedient to God by getting out of bed to go read this scripture (my Bible was in the living room) and receive my blessing or I could go back to sleep and miss out on my blessing. I chose my blessing because at that point, all I wanted was to be in the presence of the LORD. There is no other feeling like it in this world! I've been chasing God's presence ever since. My heart was renovated. I know for myself that He is real and I want you to know it too. This is what God wants you to know:

"Ye have not chosen me, but I have chosen you, and ordained you, that ye should go and bring forth fruit, and that your fruit should remain: that whatsoever ye shall ask of the Father in my name, He may give it you." – John 15:16

I AM BLESSED AND HIGHLY FAVORED

God never gives up on you. Renovate your heart today. Jesus is calling...will you answer? "If we confess our sins, He is faithful and just and will forgive our sins and purify us from all unrighteousness." – 1 John 1:9

Forgive all things. Love all people.

"Having therefore, brethren, boldness to enter into the holiest by the blood of Jesus, [20]By a new and living way, which He hath consecrated for us, through the veil, that is to say, his flesh; [21]And having an high priest over the house of God; [22]Let us draw near with a true heart in full assurance of faith, having our hearts sprinkled from an evil conscience, and our bodies washed with pure water. [23]Let us hold fast the profession of our faith without wavering; (for He is faithful that promised;)" – Hebrews 10:19-23

Living God's way requires you to be filled with His Holy Spirit so you can lovingly respect human life. Many of you respect and care for animals better than you respect and care for humans. You'd rather take in a stray animal than to care for a child in need. You say it's too costly and too time consuming to take in a child, but you regularly take your pets to the veterinarian for health care and vaccinations; you feed them a few times a day; you bathe them; you cuddle them; you take them to potty; you buy them toys and clothes; you train them and teach them; all the things required to care for a child. Dogs have become the pride of men; the idol of men. "Pride goes before destruction and haughtiness before a fall." - Proverbs 16:18 NLT

As a nation, we are a selfish people. Below are scriptures that you may consider.

"Beware of dogs, beware of evil workers, beware of the concision." – Philippians 3:2

"As a dog returns to his vomit, so a fool returns to his folly." – Proverbs 26:11

"Deliver my soul from the sword; My darling from the power of the dog." – Psalm 22:20

"Give not that which is holy unto the dogs, neither cast ye your pearls before swine, lest they trample them under their feet, and turn again and rend you." – Matthew 7:6

"For dogs have compassed me: The assembly of the wicked has inclosed me: They pierced my hands and my feet." – Psalm 22:16

"For <u>without</u> are dogs, and sorcerers, and whoremongers, and murderers, and idolaters, and whosoever loveth and maketh a lie." – Revelation 22:15

"If my people, which are called by my name, shall humble themselves, and pray, and seek my face, and turn from their wicked says; then will I hear from heaven, and will forgive their sin, and will heal their land." – 2 Chronicles 7:14

WON'T HE DO IT

Jehovah Jireh – My Provider

"But though He had done so many miracles before them, yet they believed not on Him." – John 12:37

"God also bearing them witness, both with signs and wonders, and with divers miracles, and gifts of the Holy Ghost, according to His own will?" – Hebrews 2:4

What do you think of when you hear the word miracle?

God is transcended: He is not limited by space and time.

Therefore, to you as children of the Most High God, there are no limits on miracles. Jesus is the fulfillment of God's revelations. So, you have full access and authority to His powers. Authority is not so much from what we read, but from what God's Holy Spirit communicates to us and in us. Won't He do it?

You cannot see forgiveness of sin, but you can witness miracles.

I was excited about expecting my very first bundle of joy in 1991. I was in my twenty ninth hour of labor and it seemed as though she would never make an entrance into this world. The pain was excruciating! I had given up. I cried out to God; I told Him that I give up; couldn't take it anymore. I relaxed, gave in, and gave up. Immediately my baby girl came and it was all over. I was not experiencing the joy of being a first time mother; a joy like no other.

"In my distress I called upon the LORD, and cried to my God: And He did hear my voice out of His temple, and my cry did enter into His ears." – 2 Samuel 22:7

In the year 2010 after experiencing complications during and after child birth, I made a visit to the hospital's emergency room. During this time, I was in so much pain that it hurt to hold my baby girl. I experienced continuous pain in my body for months.

While lying there on the bed, I prayed and asked God to help me. I told Him that I could no longer take the physical pain in my body or the emotional pain from an ungodly husband. I wanted to leave and I did. As my husband and the nurse conversed and I laid there in a fog waiting for God to make His move, my spirit suddenly left my body and ascended to the ceiling in the corner of the room. I was now looking down at myself. I could hear them speaking but couldn't understand everything they were saying. However, I did hear the Holy Spirit clearly. If I was ready to go and leave my newborn behind, He would take me. I recall yelling, I want to go back...I want to go back! Just as suddenly as my spirit ascended, it descended back to my body in my bed. It felt like a plunge and I felt it. I looked around, thinking I was heard and seen but I wasn't. That experience was between me and God. I'm not where I am because of me. It is because of Devine intervention.

"You are my lamp, O LORD; the LORD turns my darkness into light." – 2 Samuel 22:29

"The name of the LORD is a strong tower, the righteous run to it and are safe." – Proverbs 18:10

Over the course of my life, there have been many times when God not only showed up spiritually or physically but He showed up financially as well. I always have what I need, when I need it. I recall many times praying and asking God to make a way even when with the naked eye, I could see no way. He showed up; never leaving me nor forsaking me. A walk to the mailbox and what I needed was there. A review of my bank account and what I needed was there. God will use any one and any situation to provide for His children even when others don't realize they're being used by God. God is intentional. He has promised to provide and He does; He is faithful.

AT THE ALTAR

Jehovah Rophe – My Healer

In 2011, after having experienced arthritis in my body for 21 years, God's Holy Spirit led me to a Friday night prayer service at a local church. My mother went along with me. I spent many years taking pain pills, getting injections in the hip, rubbing on ointments, and having my family members massage by body to relieve my pain. So, I left home <u>believing in my heart that I would be healed</u>.

The church hosted a visiting Prophet from another state. As he spoke, I believed in my heart that God would heal me. When it was time to go to altar for prayer and healing, I went with full expectations of being healed. As I stood there, the pastor of the local church whispered to the Prophet and pointed out whom he wanted the Prophet to pray for. I knew this wasn't the will of God. The visiting Prophet knew it too. He displayed a look of embarrassment; a look of, this isn't the way this is supposed to be.

Meanwhile, those of us not selected, returned to our seats. However, I believed in my heart that I would be healed. I sat in my seat and with an open heart rather than a discouraged one, I was ready to receive my healing; my blessing from the LORD. I took detailed notes and recorded every scripture the Prophet referenced for healing. I went home and I read them aloud each day like he said to do. I claimed boldly and spoke loudly that pain does not live in my body, like the Prophet suggested. I spoke it aloud day and night; putting it into the atmosphere. I needed the enemy to know that I believed.

One day shortly afterward (approximately 2 months later), I was home praising the LORD through songs while doing house chores when it dawned on me that I wasn't experiencing any pain. As a matter of fact, I could not remember the last time I'd had pain. I continued praising God for He is worthy to be praised. God healed me because...I believed.

Miracles... in the name of Jesus

ANGELS ALL AROUND ME

Jehovah Nissi – My Protector

"And Jacob went on his way, and the angels of God met him." – Genesis 32:1

I saw the angels of heaven. They were of all shapes and sizes; men, women, and children, of the clouds.

In 2014, I was traveling on interstate 20 from Augusta Georgia back home to the Atlanta Metropolitan area. Upon entering my vehicle, I inserted my Jimmy Hicks "Born Blessed" CD. I began listening to the very first song – Blessed Like That. I played it over and over and over and became filled with God's Holy Spirit. I was praising God; singing and dancing in my seat while driving without concern of who was watching or what they may be thinking. Tears of joy were flowing and I was on a natural spiritual high. It was just me and the LORD.

The Holy Spirit led me to look up. I did and oh, Alleluia! Angels were all around me. My vehicle was surrounded...taken hostage by Angels of God. God showed up! The angels of the LORD protected and guided me all the way back home. The light of the LORD shone brightly all around my vehicle. The sky was lit with peace and joy and so was my heart. As I entered my driveway I looked up, said thank you Jesus, and the Angels disappeared. The LORD's will had been done in the name of Jesus.

Angels all around me

A couple of weeks after my only brother passed away, I walked outside my home onto the porch and immediately, I heard his voice telling me to "let it go." I knew what he was referring to.

Shortly after that as I overslept and was sure to miss my routine of going to the gym before work, my brother's spirit woke me up approximately 5:15 a.m. I awoke to a scratching sound on the outside of the house near my bedroom. This was the same area where my brother repaired the vinyl siding shortly before his death. It was as if he was out there working as before. I acknowledged and thanked him.

A few months later, I was lying on the sofa one night waiting for my oldest daughter to come home from her late night shift at the movie theater. I typically stayed up so I could open the door for her once I hear her pull into the driveway, to insure her safety. Unfortunately on this night I fell asleep and didn't hear when she drove up. As she put her key in the door, my deceased brother's spirit walked passed me with his suit jacket brushing across my face and waking me up. So again, I acknowledged and thanked him.

God allows His Holy Angels and His Holy Spirit to protect us. I am so grateful for this. I once attempted to change prongs on my clothes dryer. To be safe, I went to the electrical breaker box and turned off the power to the dryer before installation. Unfortunately for me, the switches in the breaker box were labeled incorrectly and I got the shock of my life. I felt it but at the same time, I didn't. I felt like I shouldn't have been alive, but I was. I was knocked back against a wall yet, I felt no pain. The incident was traumatic, yet I felt a sense of peace.

Angels all around me

Miracles...in the name of Jesus

GOD KEPT ME

El-Shaddai – God Almighty

[14] "Because he has set his love upon me, therefore will I deliver him: I will set him on high, because he has known my name. [15]He shall call upon me, and I will answer him: I will be with him in trouble; I will deliver him, and honor him. [16]With long life will I satisfy him, and show him my salvation." – Psalm 91:14-16

It was Thanksgiving evening in South Carolina. After having prepared and served dinner and enjoying time with my family, I went to bed at 8:00 p.m. because I needed to wake up at 4:00 a.m. to drive back to Atlanta for work. I was a new to the Emergency Branch Operations Division at Centers for Disease Control and Prevention (CDC), plus an emergency outbreak was going on at the time so I had to report back the day after Thanksgiving.

I didn't rest very well but I got up early and left South Carolina at 4:30 a.m. It was still dark outside at 6:00 a.m. when I found myself in the median of Interstate 20 between Augusta and Atlanta, waking up from a dose. As I awoke, I jerked the steering wheel to try and enter the highway again and began to zigzag across the interstate. Before dozing off, I recall driving at a steady speed along with most 18 wheel trucks that consistently passed. There were trees and bodies of water along that stretch of the interstate. However, as my vehicle zigzagged, there were no other vehicles around. I could see nothing but darkness. I could not gain control of my vehicle. The wheels lifted up one side at a time in a rocking back and forth motion. In reality, my vehicle should have turned over many times...but God! His Holy Spirit keep it from turning and my vehicle went backward down the only small grassy area around. It went down a steep decline on the side of the road. I was so far down that the ambulance couldn't find me own their own. God not placed me in the only safe area around but He placed me where I would not be a distraction to other drivers who could cause me more harm. I literally had to stay on the phone with the ambulance driver and let him know when it sounded like he was near me.

God kept me

He knew that I was carrying life inside of me. I didn't know but He did. I fell asleep because in addition to not getting much rest, my hemoglobin was extremely low due to me being pregnant. Yes pregnant! I learned of this blessing while being examined at the emergency room after the accident. God knew and He kept me.

No one can ever convince me of other than what I absolutely know to be true...there is a God and His Son Jesus is my Savior.

NOW I SEE

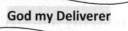

God my Deliverer

"And immediately there fell from his eyes as it had been scales: and he received sight forth with, and arose, and was baptized." – Acts 9:18

"And we, who with unveiled faces all reflect the LORD's glory, are being transformed into his likeness with ever-increasing glory, which comes from the LORD, who is the Spirit," – 2 Corinthians 3:18

One Friday evening in the summer of 2017, I was invited to a healing and deliverance service along with my daughter and son-in-law. It was life changing; all part of God's plan for me. My face was unveiled.

A visiting Prophet was the guest speaker for the weekend at a small church in Charlotte, North Carolina.

Before this evening, for so long I felt the presence of a shadow over me; it felt as if I wasn't seeing all that I was supposed to be seeing, literally. I felt the presence of a blockage in my vision. I didn't understand it until now. Dogs would chase my family and me. It felt as though heavy weights were holding me down. This Friday evening was the day that all changed. Chains were broken; scales fell off; and burdens were lifted. Healing and deliverance were offered, and I willing accepted. When the Prophet touched the top of my head, I instantly dropped to the floor. I say dropped because I had no control over my body. My limbs were without feeling: They literally were like rubber...a felling so unreal to the flesh.

I rose anew. The scales had now fallen from my eyes; I can now see clearly the way God had intended for me to see all along. I have discernment. Now I see my enemies clearly. I see their hatred for me; I see the evil of my enemies and choose to love them anyway. I am no longer burdened. I no longer live in fear of man nor creature.

I both understand and utilize the power given me by God's Holy Spirit. I understand the weapons I have at my disposal to combat the enemy's attacks.

"You will want to sing when you see what God is doing in your life, because He is your Song of victory. Just as Israel recognized her helplessness in the face of an enemy, so you must realize you will face opposition from the world, the flesh and Satan. Just as Israel recognized that God gave her a great victory (<u>Exodus 15:1</u>), so you will sing praises when you overcome your enemies. Just as Israel exalted the LORD after a victory, so you must praise Him in song when your enemy is defeated and when you win a great battle. (Exodus 15:2)" – Prime Time with God Devotion

My enemy was defeated...I sing praises to the LORD.

Now I see...Miracles, in the name of Jesus

SHUT IT OUT

Jehovah Tsidkenu – My Righteousness

"You will keep in perfect peace all who trust in you, all whose thoughts are fixed on you." – Isaiah 26:3 NLT

Sometimes you have to just shut everything else out of your life so you can hear from God. He's not a God of confusion and will not enter into mess.

"For God is not the author of confusion, but of peace, as in all churches of the saints." – 1 Corinthians 14:33

There has to be room for God to enter. If you're bogged down with burdens, stress, lies, cheating, stealing, adultery, fornication, lust, idolatry, or other sins, there is no room in your heart for God to enter. Your heart is closed to peace but opened to sin. Worldly blockages can keep you from receiving your blessings from God. These worldly blockages may include things you make idols such as television, social media, ungodly music, ungodly entertainment, drugs, alcohol, homes, vehicles, electronics, un-marital sex, people, positions, titles, clubs and organizations.

Shut It Out

In the Fall of 2017, I did just that. I shut out what was keeping me from hearing from God. I shut out television for twenty two days. I was watching shows that promote violence, adultery, lust, and same sex relationships. They had to go! I wanted to believe that I was supporting people who were just trying to make it in the world of entertainment...a trick from the devil himself. What they are actually doing is poisoning your spirits and pushing Satan's agenda. You think it's harmless until it changes your way of thinking and then your behavior. Satan is crafty; God is all knowing. I am grateful that after twenty two days of no entertainment poison, I became wise to the tricks. I don't need worldly people's influence over my life when I have Jesus...who supplies all my needs.

As I began my quest with no set amount of time to avoid television, I rose early each morning before going to work and read the word of God. During my morning commute I praised God through Holy songs; singing and dancing for the LORD. During my days at work to include lunch time, I prayed, meditated, and thanked God for His many blessings. I worshipped Him some more during my afternoon commute with more songs of praise. And before going to bed at night, I read His work some more and prayed some more. This was my routine for twenty two days without watching television.

At some point during this time, God's Holy Spirit woke me up at approximately 4:00 a.m. I awoke to God's Holy presence. I was in the presence of the Most High God. I was in His glorious light. I woke up feeling a peace like none other; something I had never experienced before. I was tired from all of my activities the day before: working, cooking, cleaning, taking care of my child, and giving God His time. At 4:00 a.m., my body was in a deep sleep; I had approximately an hour and a half left to sleep so waking up and getting up wasn't something I actually felt like doing.

God, in His greatness, shone His light on my Bible. He showed me the Gospel of John 15:16 which reads "Ye have not chosen me, but I have chosen you, and ordained you, that ye should go and bring forth fruit, and that your fruit should remain: that whatsoever ye shall ask of the Father in my name, He may give it you." – Jesus' words

These words were not shown to me. I only saw John 15:16. As tired as I was, I chose to be obedient and get up and go to the living room where my Bible was to find out what God wanted me to know. I'm so glad I did. I am glad that I did not miss out on my blessing. God was calling me. He was providing for me. He was letting me know that I don't have to want for anything! You see, all I have to do is ask my Father for what I want in the name of His Son Jesus and it will be given unto me. I love my Father; I live for Him; I live to please Him and only Him.

I shut it out and God showed Himself. The turning of the pages in the Bible was indescribable. I got a taste of just a little bit of Heaven while still here on earth. I am so grateful for having experienced being in the presence of the LORD.

Shut it out...so you too can experience blessings from the LORD.

"And a great multitude followed Him, because they saw His miracles which He did on them that were diseased." – John 6:2

YEAR OF ABUNDANT BLESSINGS

Jehovah Jireh – My Provider

"I will abundantly bless her provision: I will satisfy her poor with bread." – Psalm 132:15

In the year 2018, I was healed from the enemy's attack on my brain; I was released from personal bondage; God blessed me with a beautiful home and a 50th birthday celebration of which He would personally introduce Himself to me.

In January 2018, I began having numbness and tingling in my limbs. This went on for several days. Fearing I was having a stroke, I went to the hospital's emergency room. After a CAT scan and MRI of my brain and being physically examined by a physician, I was told that I had lesions on my brain, possibly multiple sclerosis or an early onset of dementia. The devil is a liar! I looked to the LORD from whence my help comes from; the LORD who had healed me many times before; The Lord of whom I can both depend on and trust in. You see, I understand why the enemy attacks me; God is number one in my life; I live for the LORD and I am in relationship with His Holy Spirit. So evil tries to destroy that in any way and through any one he could. At my follow up appointment with my primary care physician and after a second MRI, I was informed that the lesions that were once there are now just speckles of white spots and nothing to worry about. I call them my little angels. I serve a mighty God!

I was released from bondage. Man no longer controls my mind or my destiny...God does...Alleluia.

"And a great multitude followed Him because they saw His miracles which He did on them that were diseased." – John 6:2

In March 2018, I wanted to purchase another home for my daughter and me. Having previous experience with home purchases, I reached out to a few different real estate agents, none of whom I felt led to hire as my agent. After explaining to them what I wanted and the price I wanted it for, it was either told to me or implied that it wasn't going to happen; my expectations were too great. I received looks that said you have lost your mind if you think you're going to get that for this!

I needed a believer! I needed someone who sees as I see. They saw the impossible. I saw…my God can do anything. I saw…my God has all power in His hands. This same God who has already told me to ask for what I want in the name of Jesus.

The Holy Spirit then on a Friday night led me to do my own research. Almost instantly, God's Holy Spirit led me to my home. There was something special about the home when I saw it; there was a connection. This home was exactly what I wanted, for the price I wanted it for and what God wanted for me. The very next morning my daughter and I took a look at the outside of the home. As I drove through the peaceful serene entrance, the Holy Spirit said, this is your neighborhood. As I drove up in front of the home, God's Holy Spirit said this is your home. So with that, I called the listing agent and told him that this is my home and I look forward to seeing the inside of it. Perhaps he wasn't sure he heard correctly because his response was what? So, I explained.

The enemy did try to interrupt my home purchasing process before the actual closing but couldn't stop what God already had in place. God's plans are always victorious. The listing agent's comment to me at closing was "you did say that this is your home." God said so!

The year of abundant blessings

In November 2018, I celebrated 50 years of living here on this temporal earth. Each day that we have here with loved ones is a blessing from God. Each day that we have here is one more day to make things right with God.

Each day for a week or so before the celebration date, God through His Holy Spirit began speaking with me. Each time I stepped into the shower He spoke. As He spoke, I realized that He was giving me the words for a speech at my celebration. The more the Holy Spirit spoke I said, this sounds like a Sermon! God was calling me to preach His word. This was all a bit much to take in and I did not and would not fully understand what He expected of me until later. I went over it again and again; trying to understand it all. So I kind of put it out of my mind until it was clear, without doubt in early 2020. God was preparing me for what was to come. He is intentional in everything He does.

THE ONE WHO RAISES FROM THE DEAD

Omnipotence – God is able to do anything...He's all powerful

"And the prayer of faith will save the sick, and the LORD will <u>raise him up</u>. And if he has committed sins, he will be forgiven." – James 5:15

It was Fall, October 2019 after I fed, bathe, and put my daughter to bed. I was awake later than usual. I decided that on this night, I would stay up and watch television for a bit. I don't usually stay up beyond 9:00 p.m. for when I do, I tend to snack more than I should. During this time of year, it is hard for me to break away from watching heartfelt Christmas movies.

At approximately 10:00 p.m. I wanted a snack. The snacks in the pantry were calling my name so I made my way to the kitchen to try a new brand of organic oats and honey cereal for the first time. It had no more than a handful of ingredients so I didn't think there was anything in it I couldn't have. I ate it and then sat for about five minutes before going to bed; I know I should have waited a little longer, but I didn't. After being in bed for approximately five minutes, I began to experience distress. My throat began to close and then my heart began to swell. It literally felt like it was going to break through my skin. I could no longer breathe. This all happened within a matter of seconds. I didn't even have time to think about what to do as far as medical treatment but I knew to call on Jesus. I called on the One and only One who could help me in this desperate time of need; the One who saves; the One who delivers; the One who heals; the One who raises from the dead. I called on the name Jesus. I don't know if the word was actually verbalized but I do know that I cried out.

I don't remember anything else from that night. I typically don't sleep through the night but I remember nothing else! I do know that I called on Jesus. And I know that when I do, He answers.

I woke up the next morning and took my daughter to school not remembering what happened the night before. At approximately 9:00 a.m., the Holy Spirit reminded me of what happened and told me that I'd had an anaphylaxis allergic reaction. For those of you who are not familiar with anaphylaxis, if treatment (usually epinephrine auto-injector or epipen for short) is not received within a maximum time of thirty minutes, you die. I didn't give myself and epipen; there was no one there with me to give me an epipen. I didn't have an epipen there in bed with me; I had JESUS and I knew how to call on His name! I called on Jesus that night and the Spirit of the Living God raised me from the dead the next morning.

"But God raised him from the dead"- Acts 13:30

Satan came like a thief in the night to steal my life but God said no!

Miracles... in the name of Jesus

"Remember that Jesus Christ of the seed of David was raised from the dead according to my gospel." – 2 Timothy 2:8

"But in the Spirit of Him that raised up Jesus form the dead dwell in you, He that raised up Christ form the dead shall also quicken your mortal bodies by His Spirit that dwells in you." – Romans 8:11

The Spirit of God dwells in me.

"The Spirit of God hath made me, and the breath of the Almighty had given me life." – Job 33:4

When I wake up sometimes during the night, I often see sparkles in the air from the light of Angels. It is then that I thank God for allowing His Holy Angels and His Holy Spirit to watch over and protect my family while we sleep.

"For He shall give His Angels charge over thee, to keep thee in all thy ways." – Psalm 91:11

Miracles...in the name of Jesus

SPIRIT OF THE LIVING GOD

"For as many as are led by the Spirit of God, they are the sons of God." – Romans 8:14

"The Spirit itself bear witness with our spirit, that we are the children of God." – Romans 8:16

I was watching television one night after putting my daughter to bed. The Holy Spirit told me to go and check on her and I obeyed. I went into the bedroom where she was but didn't see her. It was dark. The lights were off in both the bedroom and the adjoining bathroom so I turned on the bedroom light and called out her name, but got no response.

I searched the rest of our home to include closets and underneath beds although it was highly unlikely that she bypassed me without my knowledge. So I started from the beginning. I went into the bedroom again; turned on the light, and called out for her but still, got no response. I took it a step further this time. I went into the adjoining bathroom because at this point, it was the only place unsearched. I turned on the light and physically walked into the toilet room where I found her sitting motionless. She was sitting in the dark. I asked her what was wrong but she didn't answer. I felt her forehead and realized she was hot from fever. I moved her to the bed and got a cool towel for her forehead. I then knelt beside the bed and told

my daughter that mommy was going to pray for her. She then spoke up in a powerful firm voice and exclaimed, no Mom! I replied with, what? So again she said, no Mom! God said that I am going to be alright.

Hearing those words and knowing the powerful God we serve, I just looked at her with gratitude. I was so grateful that she'd put her trust in the LORD. As a God fearing parent, I was elated. Then I asked, how did God tell you this? She explained that while sitting on the toilet in the dark, three Angels (older woman like her Granny, older boy about 14 years old and a young boy about age 4) visited her. She said the youngest boy held the Spirit of God in his hands. The Spirit of God asked her if she believed He could heal her and she answered yes.

My daughter and I then begin to talk and laugh about different things. We had gotten our minds off her fever and what just occurred. About thirty minutes passed before I thought about her fever. I checked her temperature and the fever was gone. My daughter was as if it never occurred; the favor of God. What a mighty God we serve!

Miracles...in the name of Jesus

"And a great multitude followed Him because they saw His miracles which He did on them that were diseased." – John 6:2

"If ye love me, keep my commandments. And I will pray the Father, and He shall give you another Comforter, that He may abide with you forever; even the Spirit of truth; whom the world cannot receive, because it seeth Him not, neither knoweth Him: but ye know Him; for He dwelleth with you, and shall be in you. I will not leave you comfortless: I will come to you." – John 14:15-18

SPIRIT OF THE LIVING GOD...FALL FRESH ON ME

THE ULTIMATE CALL

ADONAI – MY MASTER

"Ye have not chosen me, but I have chosen you, and ordained you, that ye should go and bring forth fruit and that your fruit should remain: that whatsoever ye shall ask of the Father in my name, He may give it you."

– John 15:16

GOD CALLED...I ANSWERED

In March 2020, after finishing a twenty one day fast in recognition of Lent, God made it very clear what He wanted from me. He wants me preaching His word; sharing His good news; sharing His word with His people. My uncertainty was no more. I could no longer run; I could no longer hide behind the...I'm not sure. I now know and I choose to be obedient to the LORD's calling.

I am ordained by God. Therefore, I do not need man's stamp of approval. I am chosen; I am anointed; I am ordained, not by man, but by God.

I will trust in and love Christ all the days of my life, both earthly and eternally. I don't know about you, but I have more than one life to live and my life will reflect that. Those of you who choose to live by the saying "I only have this one life to live" so that you can justify continuing in your sin, your lives reflect that.

"7I became a servant of this gospel by the gift of God's grace given me through the working of His power. 8Although I am less than the least of all the LORD's people, this grace was given me: to preach to the Gentiles the boundless riches of Christ." – Ephesians 3:7-8

God has granted us authority and power in the name of Jesus. I fully receive and trust in that power. "And Stephen, full of faith and power, did great wonders and miracles among the people." – Acts 6:8

"Strength and honour are her clothing; And she shall rejoice in time to come." – Proverbs 31:25 KJV

GOD KNEW

Omniscient – God Knows

"But I know, that even now, whatsoever thou wilt ask of God, God will give it thee." – John 11:22

During the summer of 2020 my reliable vehicle that I've had for many years began to have a slow oil leak; nothing major. I'd always taken care of the vehicle so it had taken care of me for more than ten years. I took it to the dealership and as recommended, had the valve cover gasket replaced and all was well again.

A few months later in September, my daughters and I were traveling to visit my mother and grandmother when I noticed a really nice vehicle with a for sale sign near the highway. The brand (make) of the vehicle is one that my youngest daughter and I often spoke of getting one day in the distant future. The make was the same but this particular model was an upgrade.

As I passed the vehicle, the Holy Spirit said, that's your car. Stunned, but obedient, I turned my vehicle around and went back to check it out. Keep in mind that I had no intention of purchasing a vehicle at this time, before the leading of the Holy Spirit. After turning back we stopped, looked at the vehicle and called the owner. I purchased the vehicle because the Holy Spirit told me to and I know that the LORD knows best. He is Omniscient...all knowing. You have to make room in your life for your blessings just as you have to make room in your heart to receive God. About two weeks before this day, I cleaned out my garage after months of procrastinating. I unknowingly made room for my new vehicle; my blessing from God.

I wanted to give the vehicle to my mother but I couldn't. The Holy Spirit didn't tell me to. I knew that if I did, no good would come of it because He told me this was my vehicle.

Within a month or two of purchasing this vehicle, the engine in my beloved long time vehicle died. God knew! Not only did He give me the desire of my heart but He gave me an upgrade. What a mighty God we serve.

God knew.

"Delight thyself also in the LORD; And He shall give you the desire of your heart." – Psalm 37:4

TIMES IN LIFE

Jehovah Tsidkenu – My Righteousness

"Have not I commanded you? Be strong and of a good courage; be not afraid, neither be thou dismayed: for the LORD thy God is with you wherever thou go." – Joshua 1:9

"The LORD is my Shepherd; I shall not want." – Psalm 23:1

There are times in life when I need encouragement from my Shepherd.

It is on these days that God shows up; revealing Himself through His Holy Spirit, giving me exactly what I need. It may be through songs of praise; through His light shining brightly; through sudden appearances of His beautiful rainbow; or through a soft gentle stroke across my cheek. All are welcomed and are appreciated. I am grateful.

There have been times when I needed encouragement and one of my favorite Gospel channels on Pandora would begin to play...automatically...without human assistance, either on my cellular phone or on the television. This has happened even when my television was initially turned off. God's Holy Spirit turned them on and played for me exactly what <u>He knew </u>I needed to hear. One day He played five songs in a row – all of which I needed at that moment. Only our majestic God can do that! I praised and worshipped Him; He deserves the glory.

The light inside my china cabinet in my dining room comes on when God's Holy Spirit wants me to remember that He is near. If I begin to think too much about a particular situation, this light is my reminder of Him bringing me out of that dark time in my life, into His marvelous light.

"Then spoke Jesus again unto them, saying, I am the light of the world; he that follow me shall not walk in darkness, but shall have the light of life." – John 8:12

I have the light of life.

God sometimes shows me His rainbow to remind me that He is God, creator of <u>ALL</u> things and to let me know that He is well pleased with my spiritual growth.

"and lo a voice from heaven, saying, This is my beloved Son, in whom I am well pleased." – Matthew 3:17

"The LORD is well pleased for his righteousness' sake; He will magnify the law, and make it honorable." – Isaiah 42:21

Sometimes I feel the brush of a gentle stroke across my face. This is God's reminder to me that He is always near and that I am His child. You have to learn to be still and know that He is God. "Be still and know that I am God: I will be exalted

among the heathen, I will be exalted in the earth." – Psalm 46:10

Being still requires you to listen intently, and not always being so opinionated.

"[19]Wherefore, my beloved brethren, let every man be swift to hear, slow to speak, slow to wrath: [20]for the wrath of man worketh not the righteousness of God." – James 1:19-20

Learn the way of the LORD. God loves you and wants to have a personal relationship with all of His creation. God created you in His image so He always wants the very best for you. All you have to do is seek His face; drawing near to Him.

"Draw near to God, and He will draw near to you. Cleanse your hands, ye sinners; and purify your hearts, ye double minded." – James 4:8

Continuous fervent prayer and the reading of God's word will draw you near to God. It will cause you to grow in relationship with Christ and in faith. You have to pray not just with your mind, but with your heart as well; earnest effectual prayer. This will lead you to a deep devotion and love for the LORD and His word. Be committed to Christ like you are with your jobs and relationships. Be passionate about Christ like you are with your hobbies and extracurricular activities. 2 Peter 1:5-9 says "In view of all this, make every effort to respond to God's promises. Supplement your faith with a generous provision of moral excellence, and moral excellence with knowledge, and knowledge with self control, and self control with patient endurance, and patient endurance with godliness, and godliness with brotherly affection, and brotherly affection with love for everyone. The more you grow like this, the more productive and useful you will be in your knowledge of our LORD Jesus Christ. But those who fail to develop in this way are shortsighted or blind, forgetting that they have been cleansed for their old sins."

For every sin, every problem, and every temptation in your life, you have a deliverer in Jesus. He is always the answer and will always be there for you.

Your heart longs for something that only Jesus can satisfy, so seek Him.

In John 14:6 Jesus says, "I am the way, the truth, and the life: no man cometh unto the Father, but by me." John 14:6

Though it may seem as if evil thrives and at times, uncontrollable, know that God is and always will be in control of everything. He has eternal power. Trust Him through it all for He is faithful and true and protects His faithful followers...those who live to please Him; those who live by the word standards, not the world standards. Therefore, trust the Almighty, All Powerful God and remember that He tells you in Proverbs 30:5 that "Every word of God is pure: He is a shield unto them that put their trust in Him."

God's grace is sufficient. Thank your Father for grace, for mercy, and for favor over you, and let Him work His purpose in your life.

THE GLORY BELONGS TO GOD

Elohim – My Creator

"I am the LORD thy God, which have brought thee out of the land of Egypt, out of the house of bondage. ³Thou shalt have no other gods before me." – Exodus 20:2-3

"Glory to God in the highest, And on earth peace, good will toward men." – Luke 2:14

God is the highest and wants all the glory, and all the honor, and all the praises for He alone is deserving. Give God glory because no one else was or is perfect to give you salvation. Give God glory so that you can enjoy peace here on earth that He alone can give. "But my God shall supply all your need according to His riches in glory by Christ Jesus." – Philippians 4:19

The Holy Spirit is here on earth with you to help you, to lead you, and to guide you. He will direct you in the way you should go. You must glorify Him. You must praise and worship God and recognize Jesus as the Son of God. The Holy Spirit will work in your heart to show you who Jesus is, if you only ask.

Jesus said "But ye shall receive power, after that the Holy Ghost is come upon you: and ye shall be witnesses unto me both in Jerusalem, and in all Judaea, and in Samaria, and unto the uttermost part of the earth." – Acts 1:8

The Holy Spirit is a gift from God. Accept your gift today. "Every good gift comes from the Father." – James 1:7

When you allow the Holy Spirit to control your life, you will have power, peace, wisdom, understanding, and a sound mind. You can then give God the glory that He so deserves. The glory belongs to God, not you. You didn't create yourself; you didn't give yourself breath; you didn't wake yourself up this day; you neither promoted yourself nor gave yourself a job; you didn't supply those funds in your bank account; and you didn't bless yourself with the family and friends that you have.

The glory belongs to God; for He alone supplies all your needs. We are living in a time where you want to be recognized. Social Media, a trick of the devil, has fooled you into believing that you need to be recognized by other than God. We are living in a time when you are seeking to be rescued by man...anyone who promises to fulfill your dreams...a trick of the devil. You are looking for someone to save you. You are looking for someone to supply your needs. Well, I'm here to tell you, that glory belongs to God.

The glory belongs to God

You are seeking many things brothers and sisters. You are glorifying and praising and worshipping many things and many people of this sinful world. You're looking for a Savior when you already have that in Jesus. This glory belongs to God.

You've been misled. Your savior is not a celebrity; your savior is not an actor or an actress; your savior is not an entertainer; your savior is not a politician; your savior is not your husband; your savior is not your wife; your savior is not your pastor or your counselor; your savior is not your friends. That glory belongs to God. Your Savior is and always will be Jesus! Put your trust not in man or woman. Put your trust in the LORD. Glorify Him.

"But let all those that put their trust in Thee rejoice: Let them ever shout for joy, because thou defend them: let them also that love thy name be joyful in Thee. [12]For Thou, LORD, will bless the righteous; with favor will thou compass (protect) him as with a shield." – Psalm 5:11-12

The glory belongs to God

Be careful who you praise; be careful who you worship. For so long you've looked to others to rescue you. You look to everyone except the One who actually can. You look to everyone except the One who can save you and give you peace… a peace like none other; a peace that surpasses all understanding.

God can and He will give you the desires of your heart…just ask. Be obedient and follow His commands. Stop worshipping people, places, and things. Worship the LORD. The glory belongs to God.

Choose the path of life and light. Choose peace and everlasting life that the One and only true and living

God can give you. He has all power in His hands. Trust Him; glorify Him.

The glory belongs to God

Trust God and He will give you all that you need and want. He is your provider. He is your healer. He is your everything! He alone deserves glory. No one other than Him can give you all that you desire. You have superficial in the flesh. God gives you supernatural in the Spirit. God is merciful and true. He is hope for the hopeless; a father to the fatherless; food for the hungry; life to the dead in sin; a mother to the motherless; love for the unloved; wisdom for those who ask for it; a way out for those who are tempted; a way forward for those who seek Him; a hand up for those who have fallen; a light to bring you out of darkness; water for those who are spiritually dry; bread for those who are spiritually hungry; shelter in a time of storm and peace for those who trust in Him, and so much more.

God loves you so much that He gave His only begotten Son so that you may be saved.

The glory belongs to God

Trust God...one day at a time and live in His peace. God is omnipotent: He has ALL power. God is omnipresent: He is EVERYWHERE. God is omniscient: He knows ALL things. He calls you to live in His peace; to forgive and to love everyone.

The glory belongs to God

"Blessed is the man who trusts in the LORD, and whose hope is the LORD." – Jeremiah 17:7

Give thanks to the Lord, for He is your rock. Honoring God is not restricted to Easter, Thanksgiving and Christmas. You should have a praise of thanksgiving in your hearts and on your lips every day. Devoted believers and worshippers produce spiritual fruit. Let us not grow weary of doing well.

The glory belongs to God

God is all around you. We need only open our eyes and see with the eyes of a child; see with happiness and joy…the flowers, the trees, the mountains, the waters, the birds – the beauty of it all. God created it all. He is all around you. Let's not take these things for granted. God deserves the glory.

Jesus gave up His home in Heaven to come to earth to save you. You ought to be thankful for that. You ought to show how thankful you are by praising, worshipping, and glorying God.

The glory belongs to God

God shows us Grace and He has mercy on us.

"1 Corinthians 15:10 tells us "But by the grace of GOD, I am what I am: And His grace which was bestowed upon me was not in vain; but I labored more abundantly than they all; yet not I, but <u>the grace of God</u> which was with me."

The glory belongs to God

God tells us in Jeremiah 29:11 "I know the plans I have for you. Thoughts of peace and not evil, to give you an expected end (hope and a future)." God's grace and His mercies endure forever. He is perfect in everything He does. He is Almighty God.

You must be alive with Christ, living in His faith or you're dead in sin, living with Satan. Look beyond your daily issues to heavenly things. God knows what today holds and what tomorrow will bring. Trust Him! His plans are much greater than yours. No one can take away your life or anything else until the LORD's appointed time. The Most High God gives you life. Yield to His plans for your life. Accept His protection over your life and allow Him to take care of you. For He tells you in Psalm 55:22 to cast your burdens upon Him and He will take care of you.

The glory belongs to God

God consistently works out His eternal plan for His wise and Holy purpose. He brings you happiness. Once you've experienced this happiness, you will no longer waste time pursuing temporary pleasures of this temporal time here on earth. Living for the LORD will fully satisfy you. The LORD God is the greatest source of happiness. Glorify Him. He says "I am the vine, ye are the branches: He that abideth in me, and I in him, the same bringeth forth much fruit: for without Me ye can do nothing." – John 15:5

You need Jesus rather you accept Him or not. There would be no you without Him. Your greatest blessing is being near to God; in His presence. For when you are, He gives you unspeakable joy…a peace that cannot be described in words.

"Behold, God is my salvation; I will trust, and not be afraid: for the LORD JEHOVAH is my strength and my song; He also is become my salvation." – Isaiah 12:2

<u>The one who stands for Christ will likely not fall for the devil.</u> Stay true to the One and only living God of the universe.

JESUS IS CALLING…WILL YOU ANSWER HIM?

The glory belongs to God

VICTORY... in the name of JESUS

"Great is our LORD, and of great power: His understanding is infinite."
Psalm 147:5

The Glory Belongs
to
God

Evangelist Uneala is foremost, a woman of God who accepted her calling to share God's word in February 2020.

She was born Uneala Lorraine Pope to Oneal and Mildred Faye Pope in South Carolina. She is the mother of three beautiful daughters, Amber, Taliah, and Mallory Grace and to a handsome Son-in-Law, Allen. Evangelist Uneala is expecting her first grandchild this year and look forward to being called Grandma.

She enjoys studying and sharing God's word. She also enjoys cooking, traveling, crossword puzzles, adult coloring books, watching Hallmark, Christmas, and faith based movies, and game nights with family and friends. Phase 10 is her favorite game to play. Evangelist Uneala loves all and forgives all.

"He which hath begun a good work in you will perform it until the day of Jesus Christ." – Philippians 1:6

Thank you for purchasing my very first book and thereby supporting my mission to share God's word.

EvangelistUneala (YouTube)   evangelistuneala@gmail.com

Made in the USA
Monee, IL
10 September 2021